PRAYERS TO THE HOLY SPIRIT

A Year-Long Conversation

KEVIN B LEIGH

To My Wonderful
Sister, I Hope this
Inspires you

11/30/19

SavvyBrain

Proceeds to charity.

To purchase additional copies of this book for friends and family or your church, go to PrayersTo.com then click "Buy."

Researching prayers across the web is a tricky task, as many of the sites do not include the appropriate copyright and or even mention the source of the prayer. I have made a serious effort to include the author and appropriate copyright when available. And I would love to give credit where credit is due; so if you can offer insight, please contact me personally at iam@kevinleigh.com

I dedicate this to the three holiest women in my life.
First, *the late Josephine Harrington (aunt Josie), who, in my opinion, had the ear of God. I said at her funeral that she had "an EZ Pass to heaven."*
Second, *my mom Pauline Leigh. Her prayer is so connected to God that when she prays for me, I can feel it from afar.*
*And **Third**, my wife Mary who prays the rosary so often there are wear marks on the beads.*
I am a fortunate man to know them all.

GUIDE

Foreword   vii

Before we begin   xi

1. Prayer to Guide My Actions   1
2. Prayer of Consecration   4
3. The Hymn of Mael-ísu   6
4. Breathe On to Me   8
5. Prayer for the Feast of Pentecost   10
6. I Bind Myself to Thee O Holy Spirit   14
7. John Wilbur Chapman - Holy Spirit Come In   16
8. To Fill the Hearts Which Thou Hast Made   18
9. Cardinal Mercier's Prayer To The Holy Spirit   20
10. Moms Favorite Prayer   22
11. St Augustine's Prayer to the Holy Spirit   24
12. Come Holy Spirit   26
13. Power of These Gifts   28
14. You're the Boss of Me   30
15. Prayer for Light   32
16. Right Judgment In All Things   34
17. Ask and You Shall Receive   36
18. Lead, kindly Light   38
19. Truth Divine   40
20. Come Holy Spirit   42
21. With Your Strength   44
22. Hearts of the Faithful   46
23. Spirit of Wisdom   48
24. The Holy Spirit is My Super Power   50
25. Lead Me To Confidence   52
26. Healing Prayer of Surrender   54
27. Grace of the Holy Spirit   56
28. Give Me Your Orders, O Holy Spirit   58

29. The Indwelling Of the Holy Spirit　　　　60

30. Center my Pain　　　　62

31. Prayer for Healing　　　　64

32. Miraculous Prayer to the Holy Spirit　　　　66

33. The Comforter　　　　68

34. The Seven Gifts of the Holy Spirit　　　　70

35. Spirit of Truth Show Me The Way　　　　72

36. Holy Ghost Purify My Heart　　　　74

37. Holy Ghost Unit Me With God　　　　76

38. Holy Ghost Strengthen Me, Through Thy Love　　　　78

39. Holy Ghost, Seek Glory of God in all Things　　　　80

40. Holy Ghost, Show Us How to Turn Towards God　　　　82

41. Holy Ghost, Desire God Alone　　　　84

42. I Am Defaced and Deformed By Sin　　　　86

43. Come O Holy Spirit　　　　88

44. Prayer For the Poor　　　　91

45. Holy Spirit, Wake Up My Senses　　　　93

46. For Good Choices　　　　95

47. Chaplet of the Holy Ghost　　　　97

48. Light of Every Human Heart　　　　103

49. Seven Prayers of the Holy Spirit　　　　105

50. Look Inside My Heart　　　　108

51. Sacred Trinity with Mary　　　　111

52. Sweet Guest of My Soul　　　　114

Important Prayers Named Throughout　　　　117

Acknowledgments　　　　121

About the Author　　　　125

FOREWORD

*"May Christ's words be on my mind, on my lips,
and in my heart."*

Not long before his death, I received a call from my dad, a first-generation Irish immigrant, and fourth-degree Knight of Columbus. He excitedly reported to me, in his lovely Irish accent, "Kevin, I've finally found the Holy Spirit..."

"Really?" I replied sarcastically.

"Yeah, and He was right under me nose."

Now, Dad (known to all of us as simply the Da) was a little eccentric, so I didn't pay much attention to his revelation at the time. After all, I was young and still at the stage in my life where I thought my parents were sort of dumb. But, like most young adults, I came to find out that my parents were two of the smartest, most caring, and holiest people I have ever known.

For the rest of his life, the Da would invoke the Holy Spirit in almost every conversation he had with me. Encouraging me to pray **"with"** the Holy Spirit because, as he said, "The Holy Spirit is already in you."

The Da believed that it was important that **"I found the gifts that were already given to me by God at birth, especially the Holy Spirit."**

My only connection to the Holy Spirit for years after the Da's death was a small, powerful prayer he taught me. Which I say several times each day. It's so important to me that I made it the first prayer in the book.

COMMISSIONED BY THE HOLY SPIRIT

It maybe naive of me to believe that a small person such as myself in the eyes of God, could be inspired directly by the Holy Spirit. But I do believe this collection of prayers was curated and commissioned by the Holy Spirit Himself. Because in my heart of hearts, I believe this body of work was written indirectly by Him.

As I researched these prayers from sources all over the world and throughout time and history, I felt the Holy Spirit guide me as I picked, edited, and in some cases, wrote from scratch the words found on the following pages.

It's funny how from time to time you find little quotes that are relevant for the moment. That is what happened when I was writing the above section of the forward to the book. I came across a quote from mother Teresa thats in the book the Joy of Living. Here is the quote.

"I am a little pencil in God's hands. He does the thinking. He does the writing. He does everything and sometimes it is really hard because it is a broken pencil and He has to sharpen it a little more."

— Mother Teresa, The Joy in Loving: A Guide to

In my research, I would discover what I thought was a beautiful prayer, that at first appeared to be holy and Christian, but the Holy Spirit would steer me past.

He works through me in a very forceful way, sort of like a mental crack of disgust. Shuttering, I would leave the website or dizzily close the book where I found the suspect prayer. In some cases, I was urged to write the prayer I was looking for myself. With what I believe to be the Holy Spirit's Devine Guidance.

Then in other cases, I would find a prayer on a website or ancient tome that jumped off the page at me. My skin would flush, and in one case, my fitness watch notified me of a spike in my heart rate, thinking that I had a heart attack.

Was this the Holy Spirit guiding me down a path of His will? I believe so. Not because I am holy; in fact, I am just a layperson, or as one book from 1925 calls people like me, "the ordinary."

Well, there is an easy to find out; read the book yourself, and maybe if you'll feel what I felt. I hope that you find similar emotion in the words I write and the prayers I've listed. If the prayers feel right to you, please let me know. If they give you a bad feeling, let me know that too. Because if there is one thing I know for sure; there are people out there with a much stronger connections to the Holy Spirit than I.

As I've said, I am just a layperson in the church but one who continuously seeks guidance from those with more experience. Feel free to contact me. Again, the email for this project is holyspirit@kevinleigh.com

WHY 52 PRAYERS

At first, I wrote out a few small prayers in a Moleskin journal and took them to church with me each morning. But my fingers would not stop, could not stop for some reason. Before I knew it, I had collected 20, then 40. Then one for each week of the year.

I still have the feeling that my work is not done, my ultimate goal is to create a 365 prayer version. One for every day of the year.

So I ask for your help.

If you have a prayer to the Holy Spirit that you think belongs in the next book, please share it with me so I can share it with the world.

Please include its source and a little story about how it has helped you, and I will do my best to include it in future versions.

The email for this project is iam@kevinleigh.com

I honestly would love to hear from you and am grateful in advance for your help.

> *OK, let's get started on our Prayers With The Holy Spirit.*

BEFORE WE BEGIN

Lets start off by **blessing ourselves**.

In the early days of the church, we blessed ourselves using our full hand because five fingers represented the five Holy Wounds of Christ.

Now it is customary to use three fingers, believed to represent the Blessed Trinity, putting the two remaining fingers in the palm to symbolize the two natures of Christ; this is known as the Byzantine version.

CATHOLIC VERSION:

Using your right hand.

Touch your hand to your forehead.

Then move your hand down and touch the lower part of your breastbone.

Then touch your hand to your left shoulder.

Then touch your hand to your right shoulder.

Finally, end with hands together in prayer.

EASTERN CHRISTIAN VARIATION:

From top to bottom and then from right to left.

BYZANTINE TRADITION:

Hold your thumb and first two forefingers together then touch your forehead

I believe there is no wrong method, just find what is comfortable for you.

I was taught a version when I lived in Ireland that was based on the mosaic in the front of our catechisms, showing Christ Pantocrator using his first two fingers, which is believed to be the origin of the sign of peace.

PRAYER TO GUIDE MY ACTIONS

W hen I was young, my father, Noel Leigh, *shown above on Pilgrimage at Croagh Patrick*, taught me a small prayer to the Holy Spirit. He insisted that I recite it before every meeting, before every major conversation and every important decision I had to make. He strongly believed that if you asked the Holy Spirit to come into you, anything was possible.

My dad's prayer to the Holy Spirit.

"Holy Spirit, come into my heart and guide my actions."

Or the Longer Version

Holy Spirit, come into my heart and guide my actions.
Holy Spirit, come into my soul and guide my spirituality.
Holy Spirit, come into my mind and guide my thoughts.

Mother Mary Pray for me. That I may use the gifts that God has given me at birth for the betterment of my family and my church.

I like to add each of the above to each decade of my rosary like this:

For those who pray different versions of the Rosary, please forgive my changes. Know that this version comes from my heart, where I believe, the Holy Spirit resides.

❧ 2 ❧

PRAYER OF CONSECRATION

These prayers are believed to be written by Father Felix de Jesus Rougier a Catholic priest and founder of several institutes of consecrated life. Who was declared venerable by Pope John Paul II.

His last words when he died in 1938 were:

"With Mary everything, without her, nothing."

Daily Consecration to the Holy Spirit

O Most Holy Spirit, receive the consecration that I make of my entire life and being.

From this moment on, come into every area of my life and into each of my actions and into all of my thoughts.

You are my Light, my Guide, my Strength, my Soul and my Heart.

I give all of myself without reserve to your divine action, and I desire to welcome into my soul your Devine inspirations.

O Holy Spirit, transform me with and through Our Blessed Mother Mary into your apostle, for the glory of the Father, the Mother, The Son Jesus and you O Holy Spirit and for the salvation of the world.

Amen.

THE HYMN OF MAEL-ÍSU

There was a time when Christianity was facing extinction through war, territorial disputes, and loss of faith. During that time, small pockets of the faithful hid away in monasteries in obscure parts of the world. Such  as on the spike island of Skellig Michael off the coast of Ireland, *pictured above,* or the Sümela Monastery, standing at the foot of a steep cliff facing the Altindere valley in modern-day Turkey.

In these places, the faithful wrote about Christ and even hand-copied the Bible over and over again to be sent into the world like a virus in an attempt to keep the word of God alive.

Unfortunately, books as you know practically self destruct over time, but for some reason, a few of the earliest have survived. One of these is the Liber Hymnorum or The Book of Hymns a collection of over 40 prayers and hymns in the ancient Irish and Latin languages. These works have been attributed to the great authors of the 5th-8th centuries, including Saint Patrick, Columba, Secundius, Ninine and Últan, the latest being Mael ísu.

The prayer you are about to read was transcribed by Mael ísu an Irish writer who died int 1086. What's interesting is that he gives credit to the Holy Spirit as it's author.

THE HYMN OF MAEL-ÍSU

The Holy Spirit around us,
in us and with us,
the Holy Spirit to us,
may it come, o Christ, suddenly!

The Holy Spirit to inhabit
our body and our soul,
to protect us speedily
against peril, against disease!

Against demons, against sins,
against hell with many evils,
O Jesus, may it sanctify us,
may Thy Spirit free us!

—The Spirit

❦ 4 ❧

BREATHE ON TO ME

I felt inspired to write this small prayer after reading various sections of the Catechism of the Catholic Church via Vitican.va.

In section two, chapter three, "I believe in the Holy Spirit." The catechism calls the Holy Spirit the Paraclete.

In my humble ignorance of the Holy Spirit, I had to look up the word Paraclete. It turns out that it literally means "the Holy Spirit as advocate or counselor" or as the Catechism says:

"he who is called to one's side." Sort of like your wingMan or best friend.

I hope you like this heartfelt prayer that poured out of me in a burst of writing, as if it needed to be released onto the page.

❦

BREATHE ON TO ME.

Holy Spirit, I ask that you breathe on to me, so that, with the Father and the Son and with You, I can become immersed in the Blessed Trinity.

Holy Spirit, enter into me as paraclete, advocate, counselor, and my Spirit of truth. Because without you I cannot comprehend the thoughts of God.

Holy Spirit, I ask that you speak through me as you have done with the profits that I may become your feet on the ground, your hands of intervention and your voice for my church.

Holy Spirit, help me understand that the Breath of the Holy Spirit is at the origin of being and the life of all creatures.

O Spirit of God, O Spirit of truth, O Paraclete and Intercessor, *come into my soul and prepare me for the time when I can join You in heaven.*
    Amen

❧ 5 ☙

PRAYER FOR THE FEAST OF
PENTECOST

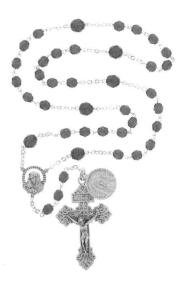

Most catholics know that a novena is a private and/or public prayer to obtain special graces. Sometimes used to ask for special favors, and/or to make special petitions.

As the definition suggests, the novena has a sense of urgency and neediness to it. For example when I first started my business I asked my mom and her friends to pray a Novena for our success.

Novena is derived from the Latin word *novem*, which, simply means nine. As in the nine days of the Novena because it should be said over the course of a nine-day period.

I use the following Novena to the Holy Spirit as a template for my novenas as it was first made at the direction of Our Lord Himself when He sent His Mom and the Apostles back to Jerusalem to await the coming of the Holy Ghost on the first Pentecost.

I think EWTN.com said it best "The Novena to the Holy Spirit is the prototype of all novenas."

Next to the novena to Our Lady of Fatima, this is my personal favorite. I hope you find Him in the following words.

❦

PRAYER FOR THE FEAST OF PENTECOST

O Holy Spirit, O my God, I adore Thee, and acknowledge, here in Thy divine presence, that I am nothing and can do nothing without Thee. Come, great Paraclete, Thou father of the poor, Thou comforter the best, fulfill the promise of our blessed Savior, Who would not leave us orphans, and come into the mind and the heart of Thy poor, unworthy creature, as Thou didst descend on the sacred day of Pentecost on the holy Mother of Jesus and on His first disciples.

Grant that I may participate in those gifts which Thou didst communicate to them so wonderfully, and with so much mercy and generosity. Take from my heart whatever is not pleasing to Thee, and make of it a worthy dwelling-place for Thyself.

Illumine my mind, that I may see and understand the things that are for my eternal good. Inflame my heart with pure love of Thee, that I may be cleansed from the cross of all inordinate attachments, and that my whole life may be hidden with Jesus in God. Strengthen my will, that I may be made conformable to Thy divine will, and be guided by Thy holy inspirations. Aid me by Thy grace to practice the divine lessons of humility, poverty, obedience, and contempt of the world, which Jesus taught us in His mortal life.

Oh, rend the heavens, and come down, consoling Spirit! that inspired and encouraged by Thee, I may faithfully comply with the duties of my state, carry my daily cross most patiently, and endeavor to accomplish the divine will with the utmost perfection. Spirit of love! Spirit of purity! Spirit of peace! Sanctify my soul more and more, and give me that heavenly peace which the world cannot give. Bless our Holy Father the Pope, bless the Church, bless our bishops, our priests, all Religious Orders, and all the faithful, that they may be filled with the spirit of Christ and labor earnestly for the spread of His kingdom.

O Holy Spirit, Thou Giver of every good and perfect gift, grant me, I beseech Thee, the intentions of this novena. May Thy will be done in me and through me. Mayest Thou be praised and glorified forevermore!

Amen.

Original text found in "With God a book of prayers and reflections" by Francis Xavier Lasance 1911

Full Printable Version:

Please go to Prayersto.com and Click on "Free Stuff" for several lovely printable PDF's of the full nine day prayer provided by churches around the world.

I BIND MYSELF TO THEE O HOLY SPIRIT

I was taught that I should trust my gut instincts. Malcom Gladwell called the gut instinct, "Blink" in his famous book of the same name. The idea you do your best thinking when you don't think at all.

When I was young I tended to mistrust my gut feelings, dismissing them as foolish or unactionable. But as I aged I realized that my gut feelings, the pull towards an idea or person is actually the Holy Spirit guiding me on the path He has chosen for me.

Is it possible that gut feelings are actually faith in God? Because when I trust myself, am I not actually trusting in the Holy Spirit since He lives within me? Something to ponder!

Why am I talking about instinct? Because my gut feeling went on overdrive, when I stumbled upon the Liber Hymnorum and specifically the Saint Patrick Breastplate prayer. Before I knew what was happening I found myself inspired to create the prayer below.

When I read the words "I bind myself to you" I knew this is exactly what we should do with the Holy Spirit. Latch on to him like a baby to its mother and don't let go.

So here is a brand new prayer to the Holy Spirit based loosely on the original Gaelic version of Saint Patrick's Breast Plate prayer known as the *Liber Hymnorum*. I hope you like it.

༄༄༄

I BIND MYSELF TO THEE

Holy Spirit, I bind myself to You, so You will be with me, in front of me and so You can come down upon me.

Holy Spirit, I bind myself to You, so you will stand behind me and within me, at my right and at my left, in my home, and while I work.

Holy Spirit, I bind myself to You, so you are with me in my prayers, while I sleep, when I dream and when I awake.

Holy Spirit, I bind myself to You, so you will be in the heart of everyone who thinks of me, everyone who speaks to me, everyone who sees me, and every ear that hears me.

I bind myself to the Sacred Trinity, the creators of the Universe, unconditionally and fully.

In the name of the Father, Mary's Son Jesus and the Holy Spirit.

Amen.

❧ 7 ❧

JOHN WILBUR CHAPMAN - HOLY SPIRIT COME IN

I firmly believe that the Holy Spirit is like a conduit to God. When we ask the Holy Spirit to "Come In" we are asking for the blessings of the full Trinity. In my dad's prayer at the beginning of this book we ask for Him to "come into our hearts." In the Novena to the Holy Spirit, we ask Him to "come into the minds…" I Pray that the Holy Spirit comes into you.

This next poem is an excerpt from a wonderful prayer by John Wilbur Chapman a late 19th century preacher, poet and famous hymn writer.

HOLY SPIRIT COME IN

Come in, come in, O Blessed Spirit, Thy work of great blessings begin; By faith I lay hold of Thy promise, And claim complete victory over sin.

O Spirit of God and of Jesus, Blessed Trinity, come and possess My body, my soul, and my spirit, And fill me with Thy holiness.

Amen

𝕊 8 𝕊

TO FILL THE HEARTS WHICH
THOU HAST MADE

This is one of the most inspiring prayers to the Holy Spirit in this book. **"Veni Creator Spiritus"** is a fantastic hymn written in the 9th century by Rabanus Maurus a Frankish Benedictine monk.

Who later became the archbishop of Mainz (now in Germany).

Usually sung in Gregorian chant, go here bit.ly/vcshymn to listen a beautiful version.

❦

Come, Holy Spirit, Creator blest,
and in our souls take up Thy rest;
come with Thy grace and heavenly aid to fill the hearts which
Thou hast made.

O comforter, to Thee we cry,

O heavenly gift of God Most High,
O fount of life and fire of love,
and sweet anointing from above.
Thou in Thy sevenfold gifts are known;

Thou, finger of God's hand we own;
  Thou, promise of the Father,
  Thou Who dost the tongue with power imbue.
  Kindle our sense from above,
  and make our hearts o'erflow with love;

with patience firm and virtue high
  the weakness of our flesh supply.
  Far from us drive the foe we dread,
  and grant us Thy peace instead;
  so shall we not, with Thee for guide,
  turn from the path of life aside.
  Oh, may Thy grace on us bestow
  the Father and the Son to know;
  and Thee, through endless times confessed, of both the eternal
Spirit blest.

Now to the Father and the Son,
  Who rose from death, be glory given,
  with Thou, O Holy Comforter,
  henceforth by all in earth and heaven.
  Amen.

9

CARDINAL MERCIER'S PRAYER TO
THE HOLY SPIRIT

D ésiré-Félicien-François-Joseph Mercier (1851-1926) was a cardinal, a Thomist scholar (of Thomas Aquinas) and the Archbishop of Mechelen in Brussels.

He recommended that we should "quite our imagination, close our eyes to everything visible and our ears to external sound and withdraw into the sanctuary of our baptized soul which is the temple of the Holy Spirit." Once there, we should "Speak to the Holy Spirit and Say:"

O Holy Spirit Beloved of my soul I adore you.
Enlighten me, guide me, strengthen me, and console me.
Tell me what I ought to do and command me to do it.
I promise to submit to everything that you ask of me and to accept all that you allow to happen to me.

Just show me what is your will.

Amen

MOMS FAVORITE PRAYER

The following is one of my moms favorite prayers. "The Ma" as she is known to her six children and "Nana" to her 22 grand and 19 great grandchildren.

It was written by the late Sister Geraldine Hedinger, *pictured here,* of the Monastery of Immaculate Conception in Ferdinand Indiana.

When my mom showed me this prayer I got pretty excited, because it hit a couple of hot buttons for me, especially the idea that with prayer even small ideas can become the next big thing. Through prayer anything is possible.

Thank you Sister Geraldine.

PROPELLED BY THE HOLY SPIRIT

Be Propelled by the Spirit of God within you.
   Become a hospitable and welcoming person to all.
   Develop like a mustard seed, start small and be patient because God can grow large trees from small seeds.
   Be Leaven. Be Salt. Be light.
   Make a difference.
   Amen.

ST AUGUSTINE'S PRAYER TO THE
HOLY SPIRIT

I first heard this prayer as I sat in a classroom in Drimnagh Castle Catholic School on the outskirts of Dublin Ireland. The christian brother who recited the prayer went on to inform us, in no uncertain terms, "that we should NOT ask God for things because God already knows what we need."

Recently, I found that St Augustine (the prayers author) believed the same thing. He said that we should instead acquire a deeper faith that God will provide.

I love how this prayer mentions "Breathe in me O Holy Spirit," similar to the way John 20:22 mentions "He breathed on them, 'Receive the Holy Spirit.'" at pentecost.

PRAYER TO THE HOLY SPIRIT

Breathe in me O Holy Spirit, that my thoughts may all be holy.
Act in me O Holy Spirit, that my work, too, may be holy.
Draw my heart O Holy Spirit, that I love but what is holy.
Strengthen me O Holy Spirit, to defend all that is holy.
Guard me, then, O Holy Spirit, that I always may be holy.

Amen.

✣ 12 ✣

COME HOLY SPIRIT

I searched the Catechism of the Catholic Church for references to the Holy Spirit. In section 2670-2672, it mentions this prayer which is formed from a combination or

The *Roman Missal, Pentecost Sequence and* Byzantine Liturgy, Pentecost Vespers, Troparion.

COME HOLY SPIRIT

Come Holy Spirit, renew within me the grace of my Baptism and lead me each and every day in accord with Your divine will.

I abandon myself to Your glorious care and trust in the promptings of Your presence in my life.

Amen.

POWER OF THESE GIFTS

I was unable to find the author of this inspirational prayer but again, it jumped off the page as if it had a life of its own. "Pick me, Pick me."

So this weeks prayer is, the power of these gifts.

POWER OF THESE GIFTS

Lord, you have enriched me with the strength of your word.

You have opened my mind and heart to see the wonders you have created.

You have blessed me with the gift of communication to share your divine message.

Holy Spirit, help me to understand the power of these gifts, and teach me to use them wisely.

Bless all who use their talents to communicate the Gospel.

Guide those who work in the field of communications to use their power for the good of your people.

This I ask through Jesus Christ, Our Lord. Amen

✣ 14 ✣

YOU'RE THE BOSS OF ME

When my kids were young, they'd love to say, "your not the boss of me," when I tried to get them to do something they didn't want to do.

My Boss is the Holy Spirit

Of course, my response was typical "I am your dad, and this is my house, so yeah, I am the boss of you."

We Christians are like petulant children. When we ignore the Holy Spirit, we are just like kids, proclaiming that we don't want to listen, "not the boss of me."

I think we all know that If we let the Holy Spirit lead us, guide us and yes, boss us, our life will be better for it.

As our leader, He inspires us to perform, shows us what we need to improve, comforts us, and guides so we can do our job, which is to make it to heaven.

Hopefully, this little prayer will help you let go so you can immerse yourself in the Holy Spirit.

LEAD ME ON

O divine Holy Spirit, the inspiration of the sacred writers and teachers of old, please inspire me to communicate the way of Christ to others.

O Holy Spirit, who applies the salvation of Christ to our hearts, convincing us of our sin, showing us "the things of Christ," convince me in the way of Christ, illuminate and regenerating me. Nearer, ever nearer to Thee.

O Holy Spirit, the Comforter of our church, aid to believers in prayer and breath of intercession for Jesus, direct me in duty, and sanctifies me for heaven. Baptize me with your Holy Spirit that I may be ready for your salvation.

In the name of the Father, Mary's almighty Son Jesus, and the Holy Spirit.
    Amen

✸ 15 ✸

PRAYER FOR LIGHT

I've mentioned my mom (the Ma) before in this book but I would be remiss to not mention her friends and family in the church. These women hold the fabric of their parish and parishes around the world together through prayer. I believe groups like the Legion of Mary are keeping our world intact.

This prayer was selected by a member of The Legion of Mary in the Parish of the Holy Spirit Church in Eden New York. A lovely parish struggling to remain open in a time of turmoil in our church. When you say this prayer, please think of them.

. . .

This startlingly impressive prayer with the Holy Spirit, was written by Cardinal Henry Edward Manning, the second Archbishop of Westminster England.

One of my favorite quotes from him is:

". . . God knows I would rather stand in the lowest place within the Truth, than in the highest without it. Nay, outside the Truth, the higher the worse. It is only so much more opposition to Truth, so much more propagation of falsehood."

TAKE ME AS YOUR DISCIPLE

O Holy Spirit of God, take me as your disciple. Guide me, Illuminate me, Sanctify me.

Bind my hands, that they may do no evil. Cover my eyes, that they may see it no more. Sanctify my heart, that evil may not dwell within me. You are my God.

You are my guide. Whatsoever you forbid me, I will renounce. And whatsoever you command me, in your strength I will do. Lead me then unto the fullness of your truth.

Amen

❧ 16 ☙

RIGHT JUDGMENT IN ALL
THINGS

I found this lovely prayer in a Book of Common Prayer from 1869. Written in the late 1700's by the reverend William Romaine from St Andrews in West London as a sermon.

It's an incredibly powerful prayer, and from the moment I read it, I knew it belonged in this book.

RIGHT JUDGMENT IN ALL THINGS

O almighty God who as at this time did teach the hearts of thy faithful people by the sending to them the light of thy Holy Spirit.

Send we beseech thee the same Spirit to enlighten our understandings that we may have a right judgment in all things and may his grace operate with power upon our hearts softening their hard stony nature and making them willing to obey the law of God.

and then grant that he may finish this great work by enabling us to proceed in the ways of holiness until we happily end the journey of life.

Oh may the eternal Spirit come down upon this whole congregation and enlighten and renew and strengthen every one of us in the inner man that we may now and evermore rejoice in his holy comfort through the merits of Christ Jesus our Saviour who liveth and reigneth with the Father and the Spirit three persons of equal honour and glory and dominion now and for ever.

Amen and Amen

ASK AND YOU SHALL RECEIVE

As I hunted the world over for prayers with the Holy Spirit, I came across a common theme among the authors. They all seem to ask for the **Strength**, seek HIS

Guidance, Help **Overcome** something or other, and Pray for an **Intercession**.

So I thought, why not just come right out and say it in a new prayer that asked for those qualities in me. That was when my heart started to race, and this prayer flowed from my fingers. I hope it helps you.

HOLY SPIRIT PLEASE

Holy Spirit please comfort and strengthen me in the midst of my difficulties.

Holy Spirit please teach me how to pray for my concerns and guide me in everything I do.

Holy Spirit please help me overcome my weaknesses by showing me what those weaknesses are.

Holy Spirit please intercede on my behalf to the Father when I am in need.

In the name of the Father, Mary's mighty Son Jesus and the Holy Spirit.

Amen

18

LEAD, KINDLY LIGHT

Cardinal John Henry Newman wrote this holy prayer. What's interesting is that Saint John Henry did not start as a Catholic but switched after he learned that the Roman Catholic Church was in the closest continuity with the Church that Jesus established. He was canonized as a saint in 2010 by Pope Benedict XVI.

LEAD KINDLY LIGHT

Lead, Kindly Light, amid the encircling gloom,
    Lead Thou me on;
    The night is dark, and I am far from home,
    Lead Thou me on.
    Keep Thou my feet;

I do not ask to see the distant scene;
one step enough for me.
I was not ever thus, nor prayed that
Thou shouldst lead me on;
I loved to choose and see my path; but now
Lead Thou me on.
I loved the garish day, and, spite of fears, pride ruled my
will;

remember not past years.

So long Thy power hath blessed me, sure it still
Will lead me on.
O'er moor and fen, o'er crag and torrent, till
The night is gone;
And with the morn those angel faces smile,

Which I have loved long since, and lost awhile.

19

TRUTH DIVINE

This beautiful prayer, poem, hymn was written by Samuel Longfellow, an American clergyman, and writer. Wonderful writing ran in the Longfellow family because, coincidently, Samuel is the brother of the famous poet Henry Wadsworth Longfellow.

TRUTH DIVINE

Holy Spirit, truth divine,
dawn upon this soul of mine;
Voice of God and inward light,
wake my spirit, clear my sight.

Holy Spirit, love divine,
glow within this heart of mine.

Kindle every high desire,
purify me with your fire.

Holy Spirit, power divine,
fill and nerve this will of mine.
Boldly may I always live,
bravely serve, and gladly give.

Holy Spirit, law divine,
reign within this soul of mine.
Be my law, and I shall be
firmly bound, forever free.

Holy Spirit, peace divine,
still this restless heart of mine.
Speak to calm this tossing sea,
grant me your tranquility.

Holy Spirit, joy divine,
gladden now this heart of mine.
In the desert ways I sing -
spring, O Living Water, spring!

❧ 20 ❧

COME HOLY SPIRIT

I'm guessing, most of you will recognize this prayer right away because when I Google'd it, they reported that it is posted over 10,300 times on websites all over the world, including Wikipedia.

I only rediscovered it recently while researching this book. It's peculiar sometimes how beauty is right under your nose, but we don't have the ability to see it.

I love this prayer because it can be a stand-alone and a

tack-on prayer. I love to add it to my rosary or my nightly meditations.

I believe it comes from Psalm 104:30 that describes God sending forth His Spirit and in the Nicene Creed, "all that is seen and unseen."

COME HOLY SPIRIT

Come Holy Spirit, fill the hearts of thy faithful and kindle in them the fire of thy love. Send forth thy Spirit and they shall be created. And thou shall renew the face of the earth.

Let us pray,

O, God, who by the light of the Holy Spirit, did instruct the hearts of the faithful, grant that by the same Holy Spirit we may be truly wise and ever enjoy His consolations, Through Christ Our Lord,

Amen.

WITH YOUR STRENGTH

I found this lovely simple prayer posted in 100,000's of sites all over the world; again, it is tough to figure out its origin. But if 100,000 web editors decided to post it, I think the Holy Spirit must want it out there.

I believe (unconfirmed) that it was written by the Apostles of the Holy Spirit, Cincinnati, OH.

WITH YOUR STRENGTH

Come, holy Spirit, Fill my heart with Your Holy gifts.

Let my weakness be penetrated with Your strength this very day that I may fulfill all the duties of my state conscientiously, that I may do what is right and just.

Let my charity be such as to offend no one, and hurt no one's feelings; so generous as to pardon sincerely any wrong done to me.

Assist me. O Holy Spirit, in all my trials of life, enlighten me in my ignorance, advise me in my doubts, strengthen me in my weakness, help me in all my needs, protect me in temptations, and console me in afflictions.

Graciously hear me, O Holy Spirit, and pour Your light into my heart, my soul, and my mind.

Assist me to live a holy life and to grow in goodness and grace.

Amen

🎇 22 🎇

HEARTS OF THE FAITHFUL

46

The English translation of the Prayer to the Holy Spirit is one of the most well-known Roman Catholic prayers to the Holy Spirit translated into various forms over the years. Hearts of the Faithful is a precious daily prayer to recite privately or with your family.

HEARTS OF THE FAITHFUL

Come, O Holy Spirit, fill the hearts of your faithful and enkindle in them the fire of your love.

Send forth your Spirit, and they shall be created. And you shall renew the face of the earth.

O God, who has taught the hearts of the faithful by the light of the Holy Spirit, grant that by the gift of the same Spirit we may be always be truly wise and ever rejoice in his consolation, through Christ our Lord.

Amen

❧ 23 ❧

SPIRIT OF WISDOM

This wonderful prayer is part of the 9th day of the St. Augustine of Hippo Novena. Aurelius Augustinus was born in 354 and is one of the Latin Fathers of the Church and maybe one of the essential Christian founders along with St Paul and St Luke. His teachings are responsible for a great deal of Christian thinking and has had a lasting influence on us.

He was formally recognized by the Vatican as a Doctor of the Church, an honor bestowed on only the greatest theologians of all time.

Like St Patrick, he wrote a Confessional that remains as one of the earliest insights into the life of a Christian in the 4th century.

SPIRIT OF WISDOM

Heavenly Father, we turn to you now with the intentions we hold in our hearts, as pray as St. Augustine has taught:

Spirit of Wisdom and Understanding, *enlighten my mind to perceive the mysteries of the Universe in relation to eternity.*

Spirit of Right Judgment and Courage, *guide me to make firm in my baptismal decision to follow Jesus' way of Love.*

Spirit of Knowledge and Reverence, *help me to see the lasting value of justice and mercy in my everyday dealings with others. May I respect life as I work to solve problems within my family and nation, economy and ecology.*

Spirit of God, *spark my Faith, Hope and Love into new action each day. Fill my life with Wonder and Awe in Your Presence, which penetrates all Creation.*

In Jesus Christ's name I pray, who lives and reigns with the Father and the Holy Spirit One God forever and ever.
   Amen

✺ 24 ✺

THE HOLY SPIRIT IS MY SUPER POWER

Our life is filled with hurdles: challenges that need to be accomplished, choices that need to be made, and walls that need to be torn down.

Let the Holy Spirit be your Person of influence, be your wingMan, be your Super Power.

Ask the Holy Spirit to join you in the morning, be with you throughout the day and show you the right path. He is in you for a reason, and He is there to help, you just have to ask.

BE MY SUPER POWER

Holy Spirit help me awake refreshed and ready to become a better person and encourage me to be kind and considerate of my friends and family.

Holy Spirit reveal to me the path to success in all that I try to accomplish today and guide my family and friends in all that they attempt to do.

Holy Spirit bring me joy, peace, and love in what I say and bring me the patience to handle the words that I hear.

Holy Spirit help me appreciate all the gifts that you have given me so that I might go forth and use them for good.

Amen.

25

LEAD ME TO CONFIDENCE

Our faith is under attack; some are afraid to say that they are Christians because even Saturday Night Life is making jokes about us.

While I am upset at what has happened, I am still a believer in the Blessed Trinity, the Gospel, and our Mother Church.

I believe this is the time for us to stand up and be strong for our church, be influential in our beliefs, and pray for the future of our incredible religion.

This next prayer is intended to give you the strength to stand up and be filled with the Holy Spirit; I hope it inspires you.

LEAD ME TO CONFIDENCE

Holy Spirit, lead me to confidence and courage, even in the face of opposition to my religion and beliefs.

Holy Spirit, show me that Spirit and Scripture go together so that I become dependent on the word of God in my life.

Holy Spirit, help me forget the failures of our past and claim our time with Christ in heaven.

Holy Spirit lead me to focus on Christ and the Gospel in my daily meditations.

Holy Spirit guide me to speak the truth so that my words help others find You.

Amen

26

HEALING PRAYER OF
SURRENDER

I found this little prayer in an article on womansday.com entitled "**20 Prayers for Healing That'll Bring Peace and Strength in Hard Times**" Author unknown.

HEALING PRAYER OF SURRENDER

Dear Lord, it is my will to surrender to you everything that I am and everything that I'm striving to be. I open the deepest recesses of my heart and invite Your Holy Spirit to dwell inside of me.

I offer you my life, heart, mind, body, soul, and spirit. I surrender to you my past, present, and future problems. I ask You to take hold over every aspect of my life. I surrender to You all my hurt, pain, worry, doubt, fear, and anxiety, and I ask You to wash me clean. I release everything into Your compassionate care.

Please speak to me clearly, Lord. Open my ears to hear Your voice. Open my heart to commune with You more deeply. I want to feel Your loving embrace.

Open the doors that need to be opened and close the doors that need to be closed. Please set my feet upon the straight and narrow road that leads to everlasting life.

Amen.

27

GRACE OF THE HOLY SPIRIT

T he homily is a time when a priest can truly inspire his
flock. On some occasions, their words can hit a nerve or
speak directly to our situation in life.

This is exactly what happened to me on a miserable rainy
morning in October at Saint Gabriels of our Lady of Sorrows
Church in Elma, NY. When Rev. Walter Grabowski spoke
about the Grace of God in his homily, I found myself
mesmerized. Because it opened up an old memory of a

catechism class about Sanctifying grace (the grace that stays in your soul) vs. Actual Grace (the supernatural push of encouragement from God.)

It hit me that both versions require the Holy Spirit.

After mass, I spent quite a while sitting in the church parking lot, pen in hand, writing in my Moleskine journal. The following is the result, I hope you like it.

Thank you father Walter Grabowski, for inspiring your parishioners.

꧁꧂

GRACE OF THE HOLY SPIRIT

God, please pour out your Holy Spirit on to me, so that I may feel the grace of God the Father, God the son, and his blessed Mother Mary.

O Holy Spirit, free me, cleanse me, restore me and make me new again so I may be one with the Blessed Trinity and Mother Church.

O Holy Spirit, Let your grace work within me, to build up my strength, and to give me the divine clarity only found with the presence of You in my soul.

O Holy Spirit, let peace flow through me because only in You can I find the heavenly joy that Jesus won for us on the cross.

Amen

❧ 28 ❧

GIVE ME YOUR ORDERS, O HOLY SPIRIT

I was taught this prayer as I prepared for my confirmation many years ago. The Catholic Brothers in my school were convinced, as I've said before, that the Holy Spirit is the leader (boss) of our soul. So, if we just "shut up and listen to Him and, do what we are told," we would be just fine in the eyes of God.

GIVE ME YOUR ORDERS, O HOLY SPIRIT

Oh, Holy Spirit, beloved of my soul, I adore You. Enlighten me, guide me, strengthen me, console me. Tell me what I should do. Give me Your orders. I promise to submit myself to all that You desire of me and then accept all that You permit to happen to me. Let me only know your will.

Amen.

-author unknown.

THE INDWELLING OF THE HOLY
SPIRIT

This is the second time I am using a prayer to the Holy
Spirit from Saint Augustine. A person who influenced
Christianity in a profound way through is writing, miracles

and deeds. This prayer survived almost 1600 years and continues to be read by christians all over the world.

THE INDWELLING OF THE HOLY SPIRIT

Holy Spirit, powerful Consoler, sacred Bond of the Father and the Son, Hope of the afflicted, descend into my heart and establish in it your loving dominion.

Inspire in my tepid soul the fire of Your love so that I may be wholly subject to You.

We believe that when you dwell in us, you also prepare a dwelling for the Father and the Son.

Deign, therefore, to come to me, Consoler of abandoned souls, and Protector of the needy. Help the afflicted, strengthen the weak, and support the wavering.

Come and purify me. Let no evil desire take possession of me. You love the humble and resist the proud.

Come to me, glory of the living, and hope of the dying. Lead me by your grace that I may always be pleasing to you.
    Amen.

❧ 30 ❧

CENTER MY PAIN

We often focus on our pain and personal issues, as any healthy person should. But we need look no further for help than into our own heart, where the Holy Spirit resides.

With Him you will find focus and clarity to continue on your own personal quest for physical and spiritual healing. Trust in the Grace of God.

CENTER MY PAIN

Holy Spirit, help me return my focus towards you, show me how to stop dwelling on my personal hurts and frustrations.

Help me be faithful in prayer and plan my life around You, please guide, comfort and strengthen me so that I may continue.

Show me how to look inside for the answers and guide me through my life that I may find solace in You.

Amen

❧ 31 ❧

PRAYER FOR HEALING

I would like to thank my mom's friend Maggie for bringing this prayer to my attention. This is an excerpt from the longer version of the prayer called "A Prayer for Healing of the Victims of Abuse." The hundreds of websites that have posted this prayer not one lists the author, but I believe it originated from the United States Conference of Catholic Bishops.

I trust that our church will finally put a stop to the abuse within and with the help of the Holy Spirit allow our wonderful pope, cardinals, bishops, priests and lay-catholics

the opportunity to heal our church and bring the people back
to our faith.

PRAYER FOR HEALING

*Holy Spirit, comforter of hearts, heal your people's wounds and
transform our brokenness.*

*Grant us courage and wisdom, humility and grace, so that we
may act with justice and find peace in you.*

We ask this through Christ, our Lord.

Amen.

❧ 32 ❧

MIRACULOUS PRAYER TO THE
HOLY SPIRIT

W e sometimes forget to ask God the Father to send us the Holy Spirit through his son Jesus.

Memorizing this little prayer may help. A reminder that we need to "ask and we shall receive."

I found this on the website CatholicPrayerRevival.com a lovely site for prayer. They have a download section filled with free resources to download and print.

MIRACULOUS PRAYER TO THE HOLY SPIRIT

Dear God, send to me the Holy Spirit through Your beloved Son Jesus Christ to fill my soul, to strengthen my heart and to teach me your wisdom.

I will welcome you, Holy Spirit to be my counselor, advocate and purify me so I can do the will of God.

I Jesus name
Amen

🙛 33 🙙

THE COMFORTER

This prayer Gob Smacked me in the face. By the way
Gob Smacked, is a term we Irish use to describe the
feeling of shock and awe one gets when experiencing
something   amazing.   I   was   reading   an   article   on

OurCatholicPrayers.com entitled "Holy Spirit Prayers" and, BAM I knew I needed to commit this one to memory.

I believe it is based on (John 16:7).

Note: The site listed above is a great resource for Catholics, I highly recommend it.

THE COMFORTER

May the Comforter, who proceeds from You, enlighten our minds, we beseech you, O Lord, and guide us, as Your Son has promised, into all truth.

We beseech you, O Lord, let the power of the Holy Spirit be always with us; let it mercifully purify our hearts, and safeguard us from all harm. Grant this through Christ our Lord,

Amen.

❦ 34 ❦

THE SEVEN GIFTS OF THE HOLY SPIRIT

In my research for this humble book of prayers, I kept finding this prayer posted the web, but for the life of me couldn't figure out its source.

If anyone can shed some light on its origin please shoot me an email at iam@kevinleigh.com and I will update this in later versions.

What I do know, is the gifts mentioned were referenced in the book of Isaiah (11:2). They are: wisdom, knowledge, understanding, counsel, piety, fortitude, and the fear of the Lord.

Not to actually be afraid of God but to respect His will.

THE SEVEN GIFTS OF THE HOLY SPIRIT

O Lord Jesus Christ, Who, before ascending into heaven, didst promise to send the Holy Ghost to finish Thy work in the souls of

Thy Apostles and Disciples, deign to grant the same Holy Spirit to me, that He may perfect in my soul the work of Thy grace and Thy love.

*Grant me **the Spirit of Wisdom** that I may despise the perishable things of this world and aspire only after the things that are eternal,*

*   ***the Spirit of Understanding** to enlighten my mind with the light of Thy divine truth,*

*   ***the Spirit of Counsel** that I may ever choose the surest way of pleasing God and gaining Heaven,*

*   ***the Spirit of Fortitude** that I may bear my cross with Thee, and that I may overcome with courage all the obstacles that oppose my salvation,*

*   ***the Spirit of Knowledge** that I may know God and know myself and grow perfect in the science of the Saints,*

*   ***the Spirit of Piety** that I may find the service of God sweet and amiable,*

*   ***the Spirit of Fear** that I may be filled with a loving reverence towards God, and may dread in any way to displease Him.*

Mark me, dear Lord, with the sign of Thy true disciples and animate me in all things with Thy Spirit.

*   *Amen*

✣ 35 ✣

SPIRIT OF TRUTH SHOW ME
THE WAY

I felt inspired to write this small prayer after reading a section of the Catechism of the Catholic Church on Vitican.va. Part two, Chapter three, article eight, line 116. Right after it mentions "Jesus *promises* the coming of the Holy Spirit." and "He might immediately *give* the Holy Spirit by "breathing" on his disciples?

SPIRIT OF TRUTH SHOW ME THE WAY

Oh Holy Spirit, Spirit of truth, the one who is sent by the father in Jesus name, come to me and show me the way.

Oh Holy Spirit come so that I may know you, be with me for ever and remain within me.

Oh Holy Spirit teach me everything, remind me of all that Christ said to us so I can bear witness to Him.

Oh Holy Spirit, lead me to all truth and help me glorify Christ, so he can prove the world wrong about sin, righteousness, and judgment.

Amen.

✣ 36 ✣

HOLY GHOST PURIFY MY HEART

The next seven prayers to the Holy Ghost were found in a 1940' era prayer book given to my wife by her Polish father. I've tried to keep them as close to their original form as they are amazing 'as is.'

This one is used to purify our hearts after a trail in our lives or during times of adversity.

PRAYER 1 OF 7: PURIFY MY HEART

THOU most sweet Holy Spirit true fountain of all grace.

Who on the holy day of Pentecost did so perfectly purify the hearts of the apostles from all sin, by the fire of the Divine love, that they were prepared to become an ornate dwelling place for Thee; I beseech Thee, that Thou would purify my poor heart through Thy grace, that it may appear quite pure before the eyes of God.

Amen

❧ 37 ❧

HOLY GHOST UNIT ME
WITH GOD

I love to collect old books, especially rare prayer books because they are a treasure trove of lost words to God. If you have a prayer book handed down from generation to generation, consider yourself blessed. Some of the prayers found in these books may have been recited thousands of times by the books former owners.

This one is used to unite our hearts after a trial in our lives or during times of adversity.

In my life, it has helped me in times of tears and brought forward times of joy.

PRAYER 2 OF 7: UNITE ME WITH GOD

Thou most benign Holy Ghost, who on the holy day of Pentecost didst melt the hearts of the apostles in the fire of Thy divine love so that their hearts flowed into the heart of God and were received in His Image; I beseech Thee, that by this same fire of love, my heart may be so entirely freed from all earthly thoughts that I may be converted to God and become entirely united with Him.

Amen

❧ 38 ❧

HOLY GHOST STRENGTHEN ME,
THROUGH THY LOVE

Aunt Josie and My Dad on her 80th
Birthday

M y aunt Josie, Lord rest her blessed soul was one of the holiest women I have ever known.

When she passed away, I was given her prayerbook as a gift. It is one of my most cherished holy items.

In it, I found over fifty Mass cards from the funerals she attended over the years, including my fathers. She prayed for the deceased every day, and I am eternally grateful to God for having her in my life. Together with my mom, she taught me how to pray.

Prayer three is a prayer of love, strength and patience. It is one of my favorites of the seven in this series. Thanks again Paul for preserving your tiny book of prayers for over 70 years.

PRAYER 3 OF 7: STRENGTHEN ME, THROUGH THY LOVE.

O Holy Ghost, most rich in who on the holy day of Pentecost did so inflame the hearts of the apostles that they, heretofore timid and weak and full of self love.

Became so strong and steadfast that they did not even fear to die but rather reckoned it a joy and honor to them, when they had to suffer shame and disgrace for God's sake.

I pray Thee, that Thou would strengthen me, through Thy love, against all evil, and make me steadfast in all good that I may not only patiently suffer all contradictions, but accept them joyfully.

Amen.

❧ 39 ❧

HOLY GHOST, SEEK GLORY OF GOD IN ALL THINGS

These older prayers are quaint in their use of language, while empowering the laity to find God in ways usually reserved for his apostles, popes, priests, sisters and brothers.

So the first time I read this prayer of glory, I physically shuck with the power of the Holy Spirit.

I realized instantly that honoring the glory of God in all things should be my primary goal.

Thank you Holy Spirit for coming into my heart and guiding me that day.

PRAYER 4 OF 7: SEEK GLORY OF GOD IN ALL THINGS

Most charitable Holy Ghost, who on the holy day of Pentecost did fill the hearts of the apostles so lavishly with the wine of divine love that they, being inebriated with love, forgot themselves, and desired neither honor nor advantage in their own behalf, but sought only the honor and glory of God in all things.

I beseech Thee that You would also inebriate my soul with the wine of divine love, that, in like manner, I may desire for myself neither honor nor possessions.

But seek alone the honor and glory of God in all things.
Amen.

40

HOLY GHOST, SHOW US HOW TO TURN TOWARDS GOD

E ven though this is an old prayer it is very relevant for our time of technology and digital social connectivity, distracting us from the importance of God.

May we all remember to turn off the gadgets and learn to focus on the Blessed Trinity.

PRAYER 5 OF 7: TURN TOWARDS GOD

O most brilliant Holy Ghost who on the holy day of Pentecost did so richly penetrate through and through the hearts of the apostles with heavenly sweetness that from that time no earthly joy or no human consolation could turn them away from Almighty God.

I pray Thee, that you would also fill my heart with heavenly sweetness that it may never more take pleasure in earthly joys and delights.

Amen.

41

HOLY GHOST, DESIRE GOD
ALONE

Like many of you, I still have young children at home. So please don't judge me, when I say; that no matter how hard I try, I still fear death. Not so much for myself but for my family that I would leave behind.

I do worry about the afterlife as well and if I am worthy of salvation.

This beautiful prayer helped immensely, but I still have a long way to go.

I will keep trying with the grace of God and the power of the Holy Spirit.

❦

PRAYER 6 OF 7: DESIRE GOD ALONE

O most tender and gentle Holy Ghost, who on the holy day of Pentecost did so take possession of the hearts of Your apostles and so inspire them with love for heavenly things that from inexpressible love to God they were ready, if necessary, to go to Him through a thousand deaths.

I pray Thee, to inflame my heart in such a manner with love for divine and heavenly things that from my whole heart I may desire God alone and esteem death with all its pains as nothing.

Amen.

✵ 42 ✵

I AM DEFACED AND DEFORMED
BY SIN

My interpretation of this prayer is that our goal here on earth is to become so one with the Holy Spirit that he shields our sins like a force field so we may enter heaven even as flawed as we are.

I didn't understand what was meant by defaced and deformed by sin until I asked that I may "appear beautiful and perfect in the eyes of God."

Powerful stuff.

PRAYER 7 OF 7: DEFACED AND DEFORMED BY SIN

O ever-blessed Holy Ghost, who on the holy day of Pentecost did with your seven gifts so arm and enrich the hearts of the apostles, that they appeared before God and the angels in the highest beauty and decoration.

I beseech Thee, that by your seven gifts, as with seven precious stones, you will so adorn my soul, now defaced and deformed by sin, that it may appear before the eyes of God quite beautiful and perfect.

Amen.

❧ 43 ❧

COME O HOLY SPIRIT

This tribute to the Holy Spirit is believed to have been written by Robert II, King of France, known as the Pious, (the wise)

Robert was born in the late 900's, a devout catholic, poet and hymn writer and helped found a Benedictine monastery located in Noyers.

When I read the troubled and violent history of this man I almost deleted the prayer from the book but for some reason (I suspect that Holy Spirit wanted it) I have kept it intact. Let me know what you think.

COME O HOLY SPIRIT

Come, O Holy Spirit! Lord of light!
From Your clear celestial height

Your pure beaming radiance give:
Come, You Father of the poor!
Come, with treasures which endure!
Come, You Light of all that live!

You, of all consolers best,
Visiting the troubled breast,
Post refreshing peace bestow;
You in toil are comfort sweet
Pleasant coolness in the heat;
Solace in the midst of woe.

Light immortal! Light Divine
Visit You these hearts of Yours,
And our inmost being fill:
If You take Your grace away,
Nothing pure will in man will stay;
All his good is turned to ill.

Heal our wounds - our strength renew;
On our dryness pour Your dew;
Wash the stains of guilt away:
Bend the stubborn heart and will;
Melt the frozen, warm the chill;
Guide the steps that go astray.

You, on those who evermore
You confess and You adore,
In Your sevenfold gifts, descend:

.   .   .

Give them comfort when they die;
Give them life with You on high;
Give them joys which never end.

44

PRAYER FOR THE POOR

Another lovely hymn/poem by an unknown but obviously talented author. What I love is how clear the view of how the Holy Spirit is there for the asking, "Guide the steps that go astray."

From Catholic Hymns by Henry Formby, 1853 now

LIGHT IMMORTAL, LIGHT DIVINE

Holy Spirit, Lord of light,
From Thy clear celestial height
Thy pure beaming radiance give,

Come, Thou Father of the poor,
Come with treasures which endure,
Come, Thou light of all that live.

Thou, of all consolers best,
Thou, the soul's delightful guest,
Dost refreshing peace bestow;

Thou in toil art comfort sweet,
Pleasant coolness in the heat,
Solace in the midst of woe

Light immortal, Light divine,
Visit Thou these hearts of thine,
And our inmost being fill;

If Thou take Thy grace away.
Nothing pure in man will stay—
All his good is turn'd to ill.

45

HOLY SPIRIT, WAKE UP MY SENSES

At one time in my life, I felt like I was just eeking along. Sure I said my prayers and even a rosary every so often, but I could not feel the Holy Spirit take hold of me or know he was there guiding me. I felt lost.

The power from the Holy Spirit can be elusive. Sort of a mystical rite of passage that we struggle to feel. I believe that faith has a huge part to play in our ability to welcome the Holy Spirit.

But then I read an article by of all people, Napoleon Hill, the 1930's business self help author who inspired millions of business people towards success. He suggested, and I'm paraphrasing, that we already have the abilities we need. They were given to us at birth. Given to us by God.

Maybe I didn't need to ask the Holy Spirit to come into my heart, maybe He was already there? The faith in God and myself are already present.

I just needed the faith to believe that I already had God in me.

The term "Light bulb going on" truly applied here. I quite literally felt the light turn on the moment I started to believe in myself, believe that God was already in me. (Chanting of angels singing in the background.)

I found the inspiration to create this prayer, so that I remember the Holy Spirit is close.

HOLY SPIRIT, WAKE UP MY SENSES.

With your Devine mercy and forgiveness, I pray,

*Oh God, **help me feel** the presence of the Holy Spirit in my life. In the very air I breathe, in the swaying of the trees and breath in my lungs.*

*Oh God, **help me sense** the presence of the Holy Spirit in my virtues, in my ability to forgive and the strength within me.*

*Oh God, **help me hear** the presence of the Holy Spirit in the words of the Gospel, the Homilies at Mass and the Catechism of the Church.*

Amen

❦ 46 ❦

FOR GOOD CHOICES

A gain my mom's friend Mae handed her a bunch of handwritten prayers she collected or maybe even wrote herself. I thought they were fitting, since I started this prayer book with my father's prayer asking for the Holy Spirit to come into my heart and guide my actions. I end with asking the Holy Spirit to guide my decisions and to empower me in His ways.

PLEASE GUIDE MY DECISIONS

Holy Spirit, I don't know what my future looks like. All I ask is that you fill me with your grace and guide my decisions today. Come, Spirit, and let me know that you are with me.

Holy Spirit open my eyes to the glory of the Lord. Teach me and empower me to follow Your ways.

47

CHAPLET OF THE HOLY GHOST

We recite the Chaplet of the Holy Ghost when some important decision must be made and when special spiritual help is needed. It is believed that this lovely group of prayers was composed originally in 1892 by Fr. John Mary of the Order of Friars Minor Capuchin to teach the faithful an easy way to pray to the Holy Spirit. It was approved by Pope Leo XIII in 1902.

The Chaplet of the Holy Ghost is different from the catholic rosary to mother Mary and is intended to be in regard to the Holy Ghost similar to how the Dominican Rosary is in regard to the Blessed Virgin.

It is made up of 50 prayers, one for each beed, beginning with three small size beads.

Followed by five sets of seven beads, each separated by two large or different beads.

There is a mystery for each of the five groups; the number 5 commemorating the Five Wounds of Jesus which are the fountains of grace which the Holy Ghost imparts to all men.

HOW TO PRAY THE CHAPLET OF THE HOLY SPIRIT

On the Medal:

Recollect yourself while gazing on the medal of the Holy Ghost.

On the first three beads:

1- Make the Sign of the Cross.

2- Say an Act of Contrition... (c)

3- Recite the hymn Come, Holy Spirit. (Prayer 20)

On each of the two large colored and seven smaller beads:

Announce the Mystery (below)

1. Pray an Our Father (a)

1. Pray a Hail Mary (d)

7. Pray a Glory be to the Father. (b) while meditating on the mystery.

Repeat this through the five mysteries.

During the praying of each set of seven beads, we are asked to meditate on one of the **five mysteries** (below), commemorating the **Five Wounds of Jesus** which are the fountains of grace which the Holy Ghost imparts to all men.

THE FIRST MYSTERY

By the Holy Spirit Jesus is conceived of the Blessed Virgin Mary.

The Meditation: "The Holy Ghost shall come upon thee, and the Power of the Most High shall overshadow thee; and therefore also the Holy which shall be born of thee shall be called the Son of God." [Lk. 1:35]

The Practice: Diligently implore the aid of the Divine Spirit, and Mary's intercession, to imitate the virtues of Jesus Christ, Who is the Model of virtues, so that you may be made comfortable to the image of the Son of God.

THE SECOND MYSTERY

The Spirit of the Lord rested upon Jesus when he was baptized.

The Meditation: "Jesus, being baptized, forthwith came out of the water: and lo! the heavens were opened to Him, and he saw the Spirit of God descending as a dove, and coming upon Him." [Mt. 3:16]

The Practice: Hold in the highest esteem the priceless gift of sanctifying grace, infused into your soul by the Holy Ghost in Baptism. Keep the promises to which you then pledged yourself. Increase, by constant practice, Faith, Hope, and Charity. Ever live as becometh children of God and members of God's true Church, so as to obtain, hereafter, the inheritance of heaven.

THE THIRD MYSTERY

By the Spirit is Jesus led into the desert to be tempted by the Devil.

The Meditation: "Jesus, being full of the Holy ghost, returned from the Jordan, and was led by the Spirit into the desert for the space of forty days; and was tempted by the devil." [Lk. 4:1-2]

The Practice: Be ever grateful for the sevenfold gift of the Holy Ghost bestowed upon you in Confirmation, for the spirit of wisdom and understanding, of counsel and fortitude, of knowledge and piety, and of the fear of the Lord. Faithfully yield to His Divine guidance, so that, in all the trials and temptations of life, you may act strongly, as becometh a perfect Christian and valiant soldier of Jesus Christ.

☙✠❧

THE FOURTH MYSTERY

The Holy Ghost in the Church.

The Meditation: "Suddenly there came a sound from heaven as of a mighty wind coming, and it filled the whole house where they were sitting... and they were all filled with the Holy Ghost, and began to speak... the wonderful works of God." [Acts, 2:2, 4, 11.]

The Practice: Thank God for having

made you a child of His Church which is ever animated and directed by the Divine Spirit, sent into this world for that purpose of the day of Pentecost. Hear and obey the Holy See, the infallible mouthpiece of the Holy Ghost, and the Church, the pillar and ground of truth. Uphold her doctrines, seek her interests, defend her rights.

THE FIFTH MYSTERY

The Holy Ghost in the soul of the just man and just woman.

The Meditation: "Know you not that you members are the temple of the Holy Ghost, Who is in you?" [1 Cor. 6:19] "Extinguish not the Spirit." [1 Thess. 5:19] "And grieve not the Holy Spirit of God whereby you are sealed unto the day of redemption." [Eph. 4:30]

The Practice: Be ever mindful of the Holy Ghost Who is within you, and carefully cultivate purity of soul and body. Faithfully obey His Divine Inspirations so that you may bring forth the Fruits of the Spirit - Charity, Joy, Peace, Patience, Dignity, Goodness, Long-suffering, Mildness, Faith, Modesty, Continency, Chastity.

CONCLUDE WITH:

An I believe... The Apostles Creed (f)
     as a profession of faith (g)
     Pray finally:
     ...Our Father... ...Hail Mary... ...Glory be to the Father...for the intentions of the Sovereign Pontiff.

48

LIGHT OF EVERY HUMAN HEART

The hymn *Veni Sancte Spiritus* sometimes called the "Golden Sequence," is sung mostly at Pentecost.

It is a wonderful tribute to the Holy Spirit and is believed to have been written by the archbishop of Canterbury Stephen Langton, sometime in the 13th century.

LIGHT OF EVERY HUMAN HEART

Come, O Holy Spirit, come!
    From your bright and blissful Home
    Rays of healing light impart.
    Come, Father of the poor,
    Source of gifts that will endure

Light of every human heart.
You, of all consolers best,
Of the soul, most kindly Guest,
Quickening courage do bestow.
In hard labor You are rest,
In the heat You refresh best,
And solace give in our woe.
O most blessed Light divine,
Let Your radiance in us shine,
And our inmost being fill.
Nothing good by man is thought,
Nothing right by him is wrought,
When he spurns Your gracious Will.
Cleanse our souls from sinful stain,
Lave our dryness with Your rain
Heal our wounds and mend our way.
Bend the stubborn heart and will,
Melt the frozen, warm the chill,
Guide the steps that go astray.
On the faithful who in You,
Trust with childlike piety,
Deign your sevenfold gift to send.
Give them virtue's rich increase,
Saving grace to die in peace,
Give them joys that never end.
Amen.

Go to Prayersto.com then click on "Free Stuff" to hear a beautiful version sung as a Gregorian chant

❧ 49 ❧

SEVEN PRAYERS OF THE HOLY SPIRIT

I n Saint Thomas Aquinas' *Summa Theologiae* (written 1265–1274) he wrote the standard of interpretation of the Holy Spirit. He called them "the Seven Gifts of the Holy Spirit."

My interpretation of the Seven Gifts are as follows:

Wisdom: The gift that allows you to understand things from God's point of view.

Understanding: The gift that allows you to grasp, in a small way, the essence of the truths of the Trinity

Counsel: The Gift that allows us to be directed by God so we can be saved.

Fortitude: The gift that allows a person to not be afraid to stand up for God, His truths and our Faith. This one is so important for our church right now.

Knowledge: The gift of the ability to judge correctly regarding our faith.

Piety: The gift that is principally, the perfection of the virtue of religion.

Fear of God: The Gift whereby we learn to revere God and avoid separating ourselves from Him. Or understanding the greatness and awesomeness of the Lord.

THE CATECHISM OF THE CATHOLIC CHURCH SAYS:

"They(the seven gifts) complete and perfect the virtues of those who receive them. They make the faithful docile in readily obeying divine inspirations." -CCC 1831 Vatican.va

In my opinion, the church is asking us to come full circle; basically, we need to allow the Holy Spirit to be the boss of us. We need to become docile and allow Him into our hearts so He can share His gifts.

I came up with the following seven prayers to help me

welcome the Holy Spirit's gifts into my heart. I hope they help you as well.

꧁ꕥ꧂

THE PRAYERS OF SEVEN GIFTS OF THE HOLY SPIRIT

*Holy Spirit, grant me the ability to know Thy **wisdom**, knowledge and judgement with your Devine truth.*

*Holy Spirit, grant me the gift of **understanding**, that I may penetrate the very heart of things, especially higher truths.*

*Holy Spirit, grant me the gift of **knowledge**, that I may understand the meaning of God*

*Holy Spirit, grant me the **piety** to give God the reverence he deserves so I may strengthen my relationship with Him.*

*Holy Spirit, **council** me so that I may understand God's directions so that I can be saved.*

*Holy Spirit, **fortify** my mind so I can undo evil and the firmness of mind to choose good when it is difficult to do so.*

*Holy Spirit, help me understand why I have a **Fear of God** so I can avoid separating myself from him.*

Amen

LOOK INSIDE MY HEART

We humans are under attack everyday. From fatigue, depression, financial struggles and marital problems just to name a few. Pharmaceutical companies want you to turn to them for the cure. Alcohol companies want you to find freedom with their new sugary booze. Social media and app companies what you to subscribe to their new program or method of escape.

But in my heart I believe you just have to look inside and find the Holy Spirit. Your answers are there.

"I questioned the scholars and philosophers but He was beyond their understanding. I then looked into my heart and it was there where He dwelled that I saw Him. He was nowhere else to be found." - Rumi (1270) Persian scholar.]

I think the point Rumi is making is that you only have to look inside to find the Holy Spirit. I wrote this little prayer to help remind myself of this fact

LOOK INSIDE MY HEART

O Holy Spirit, I come before you, a lost soul.

My mishaps, mistakes, struggles and heartaches have weakened me and my issues have left my spirit in a shambles. I am but a human bearing the burden of my family.

O Holy Spirit, I come before you, in need.

I ask not for new strength, but renewed strength. I ask only for the ability to lift myself up using the gifts God has already given me. Come into my mind and show me how to find the will to see the beauty of the world through my trials.

O Holy Spirit, I come before you, forsaken.

When I feel forsaken give me the wisdom to find the love in the world and in my family.

When I feel down, remind me that I am not abandoned that I just have to ask for the way.

When I feel lost, show me the path of enlightenment in your grace.

O Holy Spirit, I come before you, humble.

I know I cannot do it alone.

Holy Spirit I ask that You direct my steps as you would with a child.

Holy Spirit I ask that You lead me to hope as you would with a lost soul.

Holy Spirit I pray that you guide me to fulfillment so I can stand up tall with your strength, straight with your guidance and powerful with your grace so I can be holy.

Amen

51

SACRED TRINITY WITH MARY

Again, I am just a non-ordained ordinary member of the church, so the following observations are my own conclusions while researching the prayers for this book.

There is a common thread that runs through christian writing. Sort of a common denominator of the best writers that I have access to. It goes something like this:

Through **Jesus** we have access to the **Holy Spirit** through the **Father**.

Through the **Holy Spirit** we have access to the **Father** through his **Son Jesus**.

Through the **Father** we have access to **Jesus Christ** through the **Holy Spirit**.

Through **Mary** we have access to her **Son Jesus**, and **His Father**, and the **Holy Spirit**.

The Blessed Virgin Mary, brings the whole combination together in my mind. She was there with Jesus through his trials and tribulations, praying alongside him. I believe She is with us right now, praying alongside us, praying along with me.

The proof is the thousands of sightings, from Medjugorje Croatia to Knock Ireland, from Lezajsk Poland to Fátima Portugal or Lourdes France. So many times has she prayed along side us that National Geographic created a wonderful world map depicting the thousands of locations just in the past 500 years. For a link, go to Prayersto.com then click to "Free Stuff"

So I started to understand what most of you probably already know, I just need to include Mother Mary in my prayers and I will have the ear of God.

Praying to and with the entire combination is important for me. That is why I created this prayer to try to bring my beliefs together into a reasonable few lines. I hope you like it.

SACRED TRINITY WITH MARY

In the name of the **Father***, the* **Son** *and the* **Holy Spirit***, I ask* **Mother Mary** *to bless my prayers so that through them I maybe heard by the Sacred Trinity.*

*jesus**, please forgive my sins and call upon the* **Holy Spirit** *and* **Your Father** *in heaven to help me not sin again.*

Holy Spirit, *teach me how to connect with* **God the Father** *and* **His Son Jesus** *so that I, your unfortunate sinner, may receive the lessons of the Gospel and be saved.*

Heavenly Father*, show me the way to your* **Son Jesus***, that He may ask the* **Holy Spirit** *to breathe onto me that I maybe saved.*

I ask this in the name of the **Sacred Trinity***,* **Mother Mary***, the* **apostles***,* **saints and the holy in my church***. May my soul be saved, may my mind be cleansed and may my heart be filled with the* **Spirit of God***.*
    Amen.

52

SWEET GUEST OF MY SOUL

I found this exquisite little prayer in a book called the Raccolta from 1866. Raccolta, which means "collection" in Italian, is a book of prayers sanctioned by the Catholic Church back in 1807. Abbreviated from "Collection of Prayers and good works for which the Supreme Pontiffs have granted Holy indulgences."

I would like to thank the team at the Liturgia Latina Project for providing the full translation.

http://www.liturgialatina.org/

SWEET GUEST OF MY SOUL

Holy Spirit, sweet Guest of my soul, abide in me and grant that I may ever abide in Thee.

O Holy Spirit, Spirit of truth, come into our hearts; shed the brightness of Thy light upon the nations, that they may please Thee in unity of faith
    Amen.

IMPORTANT PRAYERS NAMED THROUGHOUT

I have included the following as a quick reference for your prayers, rosarys and chaplets.

(A) THE LORDS PRAYER

Our Father, Who art in Heaven, hallowed be Thy name; Thy Kingdom come, Thy will be done on earth as it is in Heaven.

Give us this day our daily bread; and forgive us our trespasses as we forgive those who trespass against us; and lead us not into temptation, but deliver us from evil.

Amen.

(B) THE GLORY BE

Glory be to the Father, and to the Son, and to the Holy Spirit:

As it was in the beginning, is now, and ever shall be, world without end.

Amen

(C) ACT OF CONTRITION (TRADITIONAL)

O my God, I am heartily sorry for having offended Thee, and I detest all my sins because of thy just punishments, but most of all because they offend Thee, my God, who art all good and deserving of all my love.

I firmly resolve with the help of Thy grace to sin no more and to avoid the near occasion of sin.
    Amen.

As published on vaticannews.va

(D) THE HAIL MARY

Hail Mary, full of grace.
    The Lord is with thee.
    Blessed art thou amongst women,
    and blessed is the fruit of thy womb, Jesus.

Holy Mary,
    Mother of God, pray for us sinners,
    now and at the hour of our death, Amen.

(D) THE APOSTLES' CREED

I believe in God, the Father almighty,
    creator of heaven and earth.
    I believe in Jesus Christ, his only Son, our Lord.
    He was conceived by the power of the Holy Spirit
    and born of the Virgin Mary.
    He suffered under Pontius Pilate,
    was crucified, died, and was buried.
    He descended to the dead.

On the third day he rose again.
He ascended into heaven,
and is seated at the right hand of the Father.
He will come again to judge the living and the dead.
I believe in the Holy Spirit,
the holy catholic Church,
the communion of saints,
the forgiveness of sins,
the resurrection of the body,
and the life everlasting. Amen.

ACKNOWLEDGMENTS

Image Credits:

Photo of Noel Leigh Croagh Patrick, by Kevin Leigh

Rosary graphic, created by Kevin Leigh

Photo of Fr. Félix de Jesús Rougier, source Wikipedia. CC4

Scriptorium of a Monastery, source Church of England

The Catechism Lesson by Jules-Alexis Meunier, source Wikipedia

St. Basil's Cathedral Russia

Photo by David Beale on Unsplash

Photo by KEEM IBARRA on Unsplash

Photo of Chaplet of the Holy Spirit, by Kevin Leigh

Photo by Davide Cantelli on Upsplash

Photo by David Beale on Unsplash

Photo of Cardinal Mercier, source Wikipedia,

Sister Geraldine Hedinger, Source unknown

The Four Dr's or The Western Church Painted by Gerard Seghers,

The miracle of Pentecost by Padovanino,

Throne of St. Peter, St. Peter's Basilica,

Cornfield sunrise, by Kevin Leigh

Legio Mariae, artist unknown.

William Romaine, drawing by Mary Evans,

Photo by Nathan Dumlao on unsplash

John Henry Newman by Sir John Everett Millais,

Samuel Longfellow, source Wikipedia,

Photo By Ben White on Upsplash

Our Lady of Victory National Shrine & Basilica By Kevin Leigh

Meeting of Mary and Elizabeth by Carl Heinrich Bloch

Conversion with Saint Augustin artist unknown

Pentecost by Joseph Ignaz Mildorfer

Photo by Miguel Bruna on Unsplash

Photo Stained Glass All Saints Catholic Church St. Peters, Missouri.

Photo Stained glass window at Christ Church Cathedral in Dublin,

Photo of a page of the Summa Theologiae, source wikipedia

Christ Healing the Sick, 1813, by Washington Allston

Catedral de La Plata, La Plata, Argentina by Nicolas Brigante on Upsplash

Drimnagh Castle Catholic Brother's School. 1960's unknown.

St Augustin by Sandro Botticelli

Christ Presented to the People painted by Giovanni Antonio Bazzi

Photo by John Fornander on Unsplash

Landschaft mit Verklärung Christi by Francesco Zuccarelli

Jesus and John the Baptist kneeling before God the Father during the Last Judgement.
Fresco at Paruzzaro, 1518

Mosaic detail The side chapels in the Rosary Basilica of Lourdes.

Last Judgement painted by Michelangelo, Source Wikipedia. CC4

Stephen Langton by John Thomas at Canterbury Heritage Museum

The Presentation in the Temple by Alvaro Pirez

Photo by Kevin Leigh - Catholic Childs Prayer Book from 1877, So beautiful

Photo by Kevin Leigh - Aunt Josie and My Dad on her 80th Birthday

Photo of the Key of Heaven prayer book from aunt Kate (1926), in its original gift box.
By Kevin Leigh

Photo by Kym Ellis on Unsplash

Notre Dame Des Oliviers, Murat, France.

Photo by Johannes Plenio on Unsplash

Robert II of France by Blondel

The Holy Spirit as a dove in the Annunciation, by Philippe de Champaigne, 1644

The Holy Spirit as a dove in the Heavenly Trinity joined to the Earthly Trinity through the Incarnation of the Son, by Murillo, c. 1677.

Holy Family by Gutierrez,

Photo of the Chaplet of the Holy Ghost X3 by Kevin Leigh

Images are public domain unless otherwise noted as follows

CC4 - Creative Commons Attribution-Share Alike 4.0 International

Upsplash - Crediting isn't required, but is appreciated and allows photographers to gain exposure.

Kevin Leigh. Free to distribute

ABOUT THE AUTHOR

Leigh's family immigrated to the United States from Ireland when Kevin was just 13 and Kevin has spent his adult life building a successful career in software and growth hacking, while always staying grounded in his Irish roots.

While this is his first spiritual book, Kevin Leigh is also an accomplished author and is passionate about writing and blogging. Much of his work is inspired by the stories he heard from his father on their many trips through the Irish countryside.

Proceeds to charity.
To purchase additional copies of this book for friends and family or your church, go to PrayersTo.com then click "Buy."

Kevin can be reached at:
    EMAIL: iam@kevinleigh.com
    WEB: KevinLeigh.com
    LINKEDIN: linkedin.com/in/kevinleigh
    TWITTER: twitter.com/kleigh
    FACEBOOK: facebook.com/kevinbleigh

Made in the USA
Lexington, KY
16 November 2019

57104070R00077